# THERE'S A DESERT IN MY BACKYARD!

By Walter LaPlante

Gareth Stevens
PUBLISHING

Please visit our website, www.garethstevens.com. For a free color catalog of all our high-quality books, call toll free 1-800-542-2595 or fax 1-877-542-2596.

**Library of Congress Cataloging-in-Publication Data**

Names: LaPlante, Walter, author.
Title: There's a desert in my backyard! / Walter LaPlante.
Other titles: There is a desert in my backyard
Description: New York : Gareth Stevens Publishing, [2017] | Series: Backyard biomes | Includes bibliographical references and index.
Identifiers: LCCN 2016027678| ISBN 9781482455557 (pbk. book) | ISBN 9781482455564 (6 pack) | ISBN 9781482455571 (library bound book)
Subjects: LCSH: Desert ecology–Juvenile literature. | Deserts–Juvenile literature. | Adaptation (Biology)–Juvenile literature.
Classification: LCC QH541.5.D4 L27 2017 | DDC 577.54–dc23
LC record available at https://lccn.loc.gov/2016027678

Published in 2017 by
**Gareth Stevens Publishing**
111 East 14th Street, Suite 349
New York, NY 10003

Designer: Andrea Davison-Bartolotta and Bethany Perl
Editor: Kristen Nelson

Photo credits: Cover, p. 1 Anthon Foltin/Shutterstock.com; pp. 2–24 (background texture) wongwean/Shutterstock.com; p. 5 Dubova/Shutterstock.com; pp. 7, 11, 19 (maps) Bardocz Peter/Shutterstock.com; p. 7 Adwo/Shutterstock.com, p. 9 Matyas Rehak/Shutterstock.com; p. 11 Ikpro /Shutterstock.com; p. 13 akphotoc/Shutterstock.com; p. 15 Alta Oosthuizen/Shutterstock.com; p. 17 Ingrid Curry/Shutterstock.com; p. 19 Zack Frank/Shutterstock.com; p. 21 Oleg Znamenskiy/Shutterstock.com.

Printed in the United States of America

CPSIA compliance information: Batch #CW17GS: For further information contact Gareth Stevens, New York, New York at 1-800-542-2595.

# CONTENTS

**Boldface** words appear in the glossary.

## Little Rain?

When was the last time it rained? If it doesn't rain a lot where you live, you might have a desert in your backyard! A desert is a kind of biome. A biome is a natural community of plants and animals.

About one-fifth of Earth is desert. A desert is an area where little rain falls. Most deserts get less than 10 inches (25 cm) in a year. The Atacama Desert in South America doesn't get any rain most years!

Atacama

South America

## It Gets Hot!

Some deserts are very hot in addition to being very dry. In hot, dry deserts and **semiarid** deserts, most rainfall occurs during the winter. Coastal deserts also have warm summers, but winters are cooler.

# Desert Plants

It's hard to have a backyard garden if you live in a desert! There's little water, so the plants have **adaptations** that help them live in the dry conditions. Plants in hot, dry deserts commonly grow close to the ground.

Sahara

Africa

11

Desert plants often have thick, waxy leaves meant to keep water in. Many grow wide, shallow roots to **absorb** water as soon as it falls to the ground. Others, such as cacti, are covered in **spines**! These help keep them from being eaten.

13

## Desert Animals Adapt

Desert animals have had to adapt to hot, dry conditions, too. Many are most active at night and before the sun comes up, when it's cooler. Other animals dig holes they use to hide from the heat.

15

Jackrabbits follow the shade of plants as the day passes. Some kinds of toads wait underground until it rains. Other **amphibians** speed up their **life cycle** so they grow into adults when there's more water around.

## Cold Deserts

There's also a fourth kind of desert—the cold desert! Cold deserts have short summers and long, cold winters. It does snow and rain in cold deserts, but there still isn't enough for many plants to grow. Antarctica is the largest cold desert.

Great Basin

United States

19

# Help Your Biome Home

Human activities, such as air **pollution**, are causing Earth to get warmer. Deserts could become drier and hotter, harming animals and plants living there. Keeping Earth clean and **conserving** water and other **resources** will help the biome in your backyard!

# GLOSSARY

**absorb:** to take in

**adaptation:** a change in a type of animal that makes it better able to live in its surroundings

**amphibian:** an animal that spends time on land, but must have babies and grow into an adult in water

**conserve:** to keep something from harm and not waste it

**life cycle:** the steps and changes a living thing goes through during its life

**pollution:** trash or other matter that can harm an area

**resource:** something in nature that can be used by people

**semiarid:** a somewhat dry area that has about 10 to 20 inches (25 to 50 cm) of rainfall a year

**spine:** one of many stiff, pointed parts growing from a plant

# FOR MORE INFORMATION

## BOOKS

Grady, Colin. *The Desert Biome.* New York, NY: Enslow Publishing, 2017.

Silverman, Buffy. *Let's Visit the Desert!* Minneapolis, MN: Lerner Publications, 2017.

## WEBSITES

### Desert Animals

*desertusa.com/animals.html*

See pictures and read about the animals that live in deserts in the United States.

### World Biomes

*kids.nceas.ucsb.edu/biomes/*

There are many biomes on Earth. Find out about them here!

# INDEX